## SPORTS SUPERSTARS

# JOEL EMBIID

### By Anthony K. Hewson

### WORLD BOOK

# ALL-STAR SPORTS

## Your Front Row Seat to the Games

••••••••••••••••••••••••••••••••••••

This edition is co-published by agreement between
Kaleidoscope and World Book, Inc.

Kaleidoscope Publishing, Inc.  World Book, Inc.
6012 Blue Circle Drive  180 North LaSalle St., Suite 900
Minnetonka, MN 55343 U.S.A.  Chicago IL 60601 U.S.A.

All rights reserved. No part of this book may be reproduced
in any form without written permission from the publishers.

Kaleidoscope ISBNs
978-1-64519-040-0 (library bound)
978-1-64494-195-9 (paperback)
978-1-64519-141-4 (ebook)

World Book ISBN
978-0-7166-4343-2 (library bound)

Library of Congress Control Number
2019940057

Text copyright ©2020 by Kaleidoscope Publishing, Inc.
All-Star Sports, Bigfoot Books, and associated logos are
trademarks and/or registered trademarks of Kaleidoscope
Publishing, Inc.

Printed in the United States of America.

# TABLE OF CONTENTS

**Chapter 1:** *Time to Play* ........................................ *4*

**Chapter 2:** *New to Basketball* ............................ *10*

**Chapter 3:** *Life as a Star* .................................... *16*

**Chapter 4:** *Staying on the Court* ....................... *22*

*Beyond the Book* ........................................ *28*
*Research Ninja* ........................................... *29*
*Further Resources* ..................................... *30*
*Glossary* ..................................................... *31*
*Index* ........................................................... *32*
*Photo Credits* ............................................. *32*
*About the Author* ....................................... *32*

## CHAPTER 1

# *Time to Play*

Joel Embiid went up for a three-point shot. But it was just a fake. Embiid then dribbled closer to the hoop. A defender covered him the whole time.

Embiid turned his back to the basket. Then he quickly turned back again. That left him open. He went up for a shot. **Swish**! The ball went straight through the hoop.

It was a special moment. Fans had waited years for it. Embiid was the top **draft** pick of the Philadelphia 76ers in 2014. But he missed two years with foot injuries. He was finally making his **debut** in 2016. This was his first game. He and the Sixers were playing the Oklahoma City Thunder. At last, he had scored his first points in the National Basketball Association (NBA).

**FUN FACT**
Embiid scored more points in his NBA debut than he had in any game of college basketball.

Joel Embiid was thrilled to finally make his pro debut on October 26, 2016.

Embiid led the 76ers in blocks in 2016–17 despite playing in only 31 games.

Embiid **hustled** back to play defense. Thunder star Russell Westbrook dribbled to the hoop. He beat his defender. Embiid moved over to help. Westbrook put up a floating shot. Embiid jumped and slapped the ball away. Some fans jumped out of their seats to cheer Embiid. Embiid's teammate picked up the ball. The Sixers then started the next play.

Embiid is 7 feet (2.13 m) tall. He is taller than many other players. That helps him block a lot of shots. It is one of the things that makes Embiid a great player.

Embiid had an open run to the basket in the third quarter. He received the pass. Then he turned to go up for a shot. But a defender fouled him right away. Embiid fell to the floor. Fans watched closely. They hoped he was not hurt again. But he quickly got back on his feet. The arena breathed a sigh of relief.

The 76ers lost 103–97. But the fans left excited. They had waited two years for Embiid to be healthy. They finally saw what he could do. They could not wait to see more.

# CAREER STATS

**Through the 2018–19 season**

| | |
|---|---|
| **GAMES PLAYED** | 158 |
| **POINTS PER GAME** | 24.3 |
| **REBOUNDS PER GAME** | 11.4 |
| **SHOOTING PERCENTAGE** | .481 |
| **BLOCKS PER GAME** | 2.0 |

**CHAPTER 2**

# New to Basketball

The gym was home for Joel Embiid. But growing up in Cameroon, volleyball was his sport. Joel would go to volleyball practice and work on his game. He thought he could be a pro one day. But his mind was on basketball. He practiced shooting baskets with the volleyball.

*Joel was born in Yaoundé, the capital city of Cameroon.*

Joel was born in Cameroon on March 16, 1994. He grew to be 6-foot-9 (2.1 m) by the age of 15. That was when he decided to try basketball. He got a video of NBA star Hakeem Olajuwon. Joel studied the video. He copied all Olajuwon's moves.

Luc Mbah a Moute (right) was the second Cameroonian drafted in the NBA. Joel was third.

12

Joel's father did not want him playing basketball. He wanted him to be a volleyball pro. But Joel was discovered by Luc Mbah a Moute. He played in the NBA. And he was also from Cameroon. He saw Joel play and knew he could be a star. Joel's father let him play basketball.

Joel had to make a tough choice. He had to move to the United States. That was the best place to learn basketball. At 16, with tears in his eyes, he left home. He played high school basketball in Florida. Joel did not have all the skills at first. Other players laughed at him. But coaches believed in Joel. They thought he could play college basketball.

# Where Embiid Has Been

1. **Yaoundé, Cameroon:** Embiid was born here.

2. **Gainesville, Florida:** Embiid moved here to play high school basketball.

3. **Lawrence, Kansas:** Embiid spent a year here playing for the University of Kansas.

4. **Philadelphia, Pennsylvania:** The 76ers drafted Embiid in 2014.

5. **Los Angeles, California:** Embiid played in his first NBA All-Star Game here in 2018.

6. **Miami, Florida:** Embiid played his first playoff game here in 2018.

Joel was a top **recruit** by the time he was a senior. The University of Kansas basketball coaches wanted Joel to play for them. So did other schools. But Joel chose Kansas. Kansas is one of the best college basketball teams in the country.

Joel was good in college because he was quick. Not many players his size could move as quickly as he did. That let him get past defenders and score easy baskets.

Joel injured his back near the end of the 2013–14 season. He missed all of the **postseason** with the injury. Joel chose to enter the NBA Draft anyway. The injury didn't stop teams from believing he was a top pick.

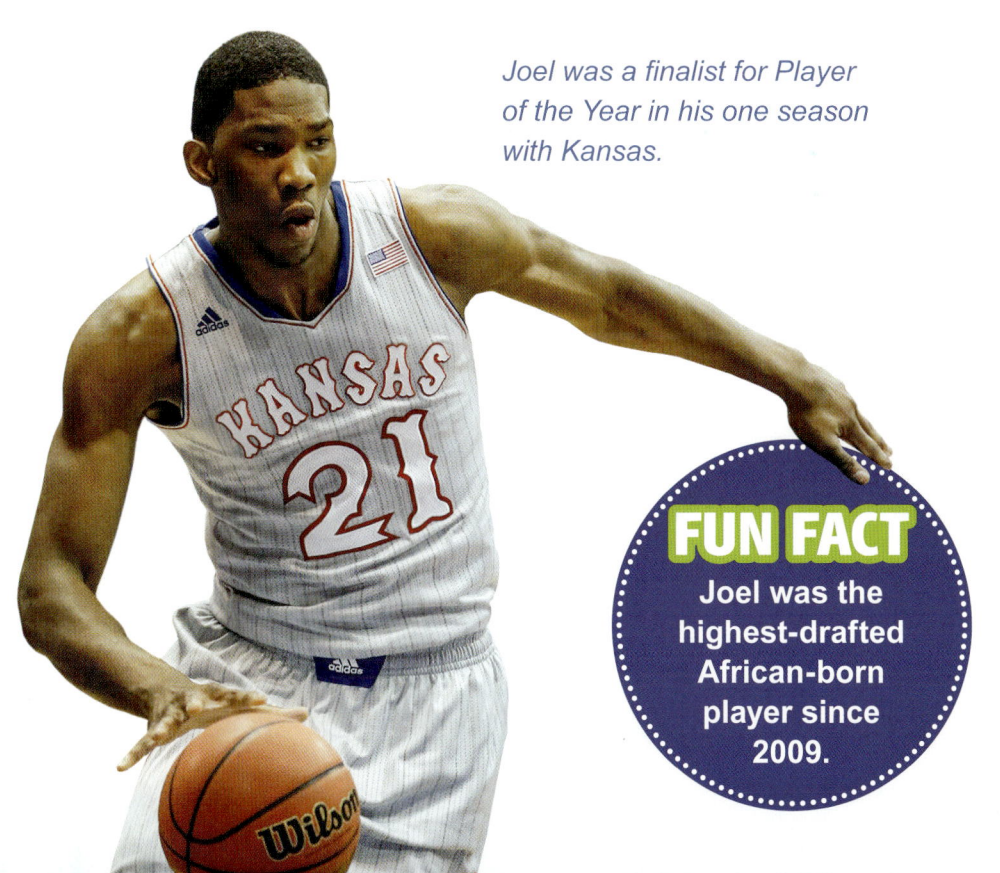

*Joel was a finalist for Player of the Year in his one season with Kansas.*

### FUN FACT
Joel was the highest-drafted African-born player since 2009.

## CHAPTER 3

# *Life as a Star*

Joel Embiid had his back to the opponent. He dribbled while backing into the defender. Soon, Embiid spun around. He got to the hoop. He threw down a monstrous dunk. The other players went crazy when they saw Embiid dunk.

Embiid was in South Africa. He was working with young basketball players there at a basketball camp. Sometimes he got in the game himself. Embiid remembered when he was a kid. He learned a lot watching NBA players. He wanted to do the same for the kids.

*Embiid helps paint a house for charity while in South Africa.*

### FUN FACT
Embiid can speak three languages. He speaks English, French, and Basaa. Basaa is a language of Cameroon.

17

*Embiid tosses balls to fans while playing in the NBA Africa Game in 2018.*

Embiid returns to Africa when he can. It was a tough decision to leave home. But now that he is a big star, he earns a lot of money. That helps him go back home during the **offseason**.

Embiid likes to talk about his home. He wants to grow basketball in Africa. The NBA held an Africa Game in 2017 and 2018. A team of African players faced off against the rest of the world. Embiid was hurt in 2017. But he played in 2018. Embiid also took part in charity activities. Embiid plans to return to Africa every year.

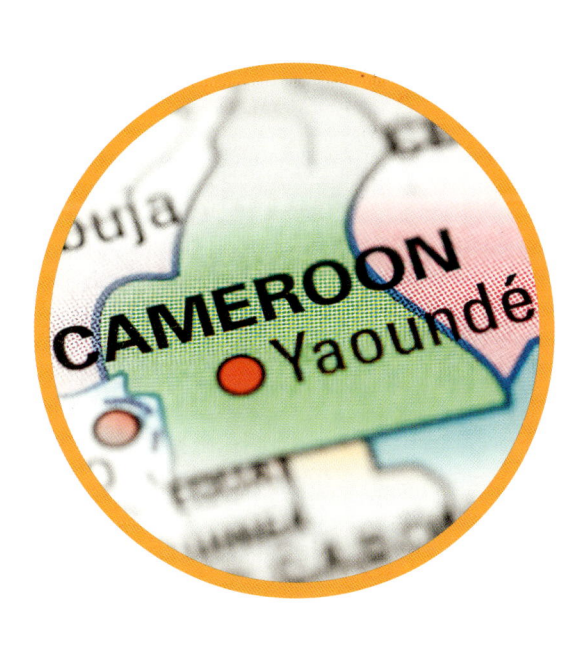

Embiid is very **competitive**. He likes to play anything, even if it's not basketball. Embiid is a big tennis fan. It was late one night in October 2017. Embiid wanted to play tennis. So he headed to a local court to play. Fans took video of his late-night game.

Embiid is popular with fans on social media. He makes fun of his opponents. He has more than one million followers on Twitter. In 2018, he played with the 76ers in China. Hundreds of fans followed Embiid around. He's known by basketball fans around the world.

# CAREER TIMELINE

**1994**

*March 16, 1994*
Joel Embiid is born in Yaoundé, Cameroon.

*2011*
Luc Mbah a Moute sees Embiid at a basketball camp in Africa and encourages him to pursue a pro basketball career.

**2011**

**2013**

*2013*
Embiid attends the University of Kansas for one season and plays for the basketball team.

*June 26, 2014*
The Philadelphia 76ers take Embiid with the third overall pick in the draft.

**2014**

**2016**

*October 26, 2016*
Embiid makes his NBA debut after missing two seasons with foot injuries.

*February 18, 2018*
Embiid scores 19 points in his first NBA All-Star Game appearance.

**2018**

*April 19, 2018*
Embiid scores 23 points in his first playoff game against the Miami Heat.

**CHAPTER 4**

# Staying on the Court

Embiid sat near the bench. He cheered on his teammates. But there was not much to cheer for. The 76ers were losing once again. All Embiid could do was watch.

Embiid didn't play either of his first two seasons in the NBA. He was recovering from foot injuries. The 76ers were one of the worst teams in the league without Embiid.

## THE PROCESS

**Embiid was drafted by the 76ers in 2014. The team's motto was "Trust the Process." Philadelphia brought in many young players. They would then get better and better over the years. One of those young players was Embiid. He was one of the best young players they drafted. That led to Embiid's nickname: "The Process."**

*Embiid was forced to spend his first two NBA seasons watching from the bench.*

Opponents better look out below when Embiid goes up for a dunk.

Embiid was finally healthy by 2016. And he was tough to stop. He was good at shooting the ball from far away. And he was good at stopping shots, too. He made it hard for opponents to get to the hoop. This was the Embiid people were waiting for.

Embiid looked like a star by November. The Sixers played the Phoenix Suns. Embiid found himself open for a shot. He stood behind the three-point line. He threw up a shot. Swish! The crowd roared with excitement.

Embiid got back on defense. He waited around the rim. He saw a shot go up a few feet away. He took two long steps. Then he swatted the ball into the crowd.

*The Wells Fargo Center in Philadelphia*

By 2018, Embiid led the Sixers back to the playoffs. But he almost didn't get to play. Embiid hurt his eye during the regular season. He missed the first two games of the playoffs. But that was enough time off. Embiid took the court for Game 3. He wore a protective mask.

*Even with a protective mask, Embiid fought to lead his team in the 2018 playoffs.*

The mask fogged up at times during the game. It made it tough to see. But Embiid still scored 23 points in a win.

Embiid has had injuries during his basketball career. But he hasn't let those injuries stop him. He has become a good shooter for such a tall player. He also continues to be a tough man to beat on defense. These skills have made Embiid a **dominant** NBA player.

**FUN FACT**
Embiid played in a career-high 64 games in 2018–19.

# BEYOND
# THE BOOK

After reading the book, it's time to think about what you learned. Try the following exercises to jumpstart your ideas.

## THINK

**THAT'S NEWS TO ME.** Joel Embiid decided when he was in high school to move to the United States to play basketball. How might news sources be able to fill in more detail about this? What new information could you find in news articles? Where could you go to find those sources?

## CREATE

**SHARPEN YOUR RESEARCH SKILLS.** Joel Embiid and Luc Mbah a Moute are two NBA players from Cameroon. Where could you go in the library to find more information about NBA players from Cameroon? Who could you talk to who might know more? Create a research plan. Write a paragraph about your next steps.

## SHARE

**SUM IT UP.** Write one paragraph summarizing the important points from this book. Make sure it's in your own words. Don't just copy what is in the text. Share the paragraph with a classmate. Does your classmate have any comments about the summary? Does he or she have additional questions about Embiid?

## GROW

**REAL-LIFE RESEARCH.** What places could you visit to learn more about Joel Embiid? What other things could you learn while you were there?

# RESEARCH NINJA

Visit *www.ninjaresearcher.com/0400* to learn how to take your research skills and book report writing to the next level!

## RESEARCH

**DIGITAL LITERACY TOOLS**

### SEARCH LIKE A PRO
Learn about how to use search engines to find useful websites.

### FACT OR FAKE?
Discover how you can tell a trusted website from an untrustworthy resource.

### TEXT DETECTIVE
Explore how to zero in on the information you need most.

### SHOW YOUR WORK
Research responsibly—learn how to cite sources.

## WRITE

### GET TO THE POINT
Learn how to express your main ideas.

### PLAN OF ATTACK
Learn prewriting exercises and create an outline.

**DOWNLOADABLE REPORT FORMS**

# Further Resources

**BOOKS**

DeMocker, Michael. *Joel Embiid*. Purple Toad Publishing, Inc., 2019.

Gigliotti, Jim. *Philadelphia 76ers*. The Child's World, 2019.

Goodman, Michael E. *Philadelphia 76ers*. Creative Education, 2018.

**WEBSITES**

FACTSURFER

Factsurfer.com gives you a safe, fun way to find more information.

1. Go to www.factsurfer.com.
2. Enter "Joel Embiid" into the search box and click.
3. Select your book cover to see a list of related websites.

# *Glossary*

**competitive:** To be competitive means trying to be as good as or better than someone else. Embiid is very competitive in any sport he plays.

**debut:** A debut is the first appearance of something. Embiid made his NBA debut in the 2016–17 season.

**dominant:** To be dominant means to be one of the best at something. Embiid is a dominant NBA player.

**draft:** Sports teams use a draft to choose new players to play for them. The Philadelphia 76ers took Embiid with the third pick in the draft.

**hustled:** Hustled means ran quickly. Embiid hustled back down the floor to play defense.

**offseason:** In sports, the offseason is when a team is not playing games. Embiid went back to visit family in Cameroon during the offseason.

**postseason:** The postseason is the games after the regular season that decide a champion. Embiid played his first postseason game in 2018.

**recruit:** A recruit is someone a college tries to get to attend the school. Embiid was a top recruit in high school.

**swish:** A swish is when a basketball goes through the basket without touching the rim. Embiid's three-point shot went straight through the hoop. Swish!

# *Index*

Africa, 15–16, 19, 21

Basaa language, 17

Cameroon, 10–11, 13–14, 17, 21

English language, 17

French language, 17

injuries, 4, 8, 15, 19, 21–22, 26–27

Mbah a Moute, Luc, 13, 21

NBA Africa Game, 19

NBA Draft, 4, 14–15, 21–22

Olajuwon, Hakeem, 11

Philadelphia 76ers, 4, 7–8, 14, 20–22, 25–26

South Africa, 16

tennis, 20

Twitter, 20

United States, 13

University of Kansas, 14–15, 21

volleyball, 10, 13

## PHOTO CREDITS

The images in this book are reproduced through the courtesy of: Chris Szagola/AP Images, front cover (center), pp. 5, 6, 9 (Joel Embiid), 24; Mark. J. Terrill/AP Images, front cover (right), pp. 3, 12; Oleksii Sidorov/Shutterstock Images, front cover (background top); Torsak Thammachote/Shutterstock Images, front cover (background bottom); PhotoProCorp/Shutterstock Images, p. 7; CBrocreative/Shutterstock Images, p. 8; Red Line Editorial, pp. 9 (chart), 14, 21 (timeline); Homo Cosmicos/Shutterstock Images, pp. 10–11; Creative Photo Corner/Shutterstock Images, pp. 13, 21 (flag); Orlin Wagner/AP Images, p. 15; Rushay/Shutterstock Images, p. 16; Themba Hadebe/AP Images, pp. 17, 18–19; sevenMaps7/Shutterstock Images, p. 19; Rawpixel.com/Shutterstock Images, p. 20; Lightspring/Shutterstock Images, p. 21 (basketball), 27; Michael Perez/AP Images, p. 23; Aspen Photo/Shutterstock Images, p. 25; Kyle Ross/Icon Sportswire/AP Images, p. 26; dnaveh/Shutterstock Images, p. 30.

## ABOUT THE AUTHOR

Anthony K. Hewson is a freelance writer originally from San Diego, now living in the Bay Area with his wife and their two dogs.